The Smart Soul

Discover Your Internal Guidance System®
Transform Anxiety into Fulfillment and Success

Zen DeBrücke

Copyright © 2010 Zen DeBrücke.

All rights reserved. No portion of this book may be reproduced mechanically, electronically, or by any other means, including photocopying, without written permission of the publisher. It is illegal to copy this book, post it to a website, or distribute it by any other means without permission from the publisher. Internal Guidance System® and IGS® are registered trademarks of Zen DeBrücke.

Printed in U.S.A.

Zen DeBrücke
Smart Soul Academy
Boulder, CO 80305
(415) 624-4866
Info@smartsoul.com
www.smartsoulacademy.com

Limits of Liability and Disclaimer of Warranty

The author and publisher shall not be liable for your misuse of this material. This book is strictly for informational and educational purposes.

Warning – Disclaimer

The purpose of this book is to educate and entertain. The author and/or publisher do not guarantee that anyone following these techniques, suggestions, tips, ideas, or strategies will become successful. The author and/or publisher shall have neither liability nor responsibility to anyone with respect to any loss or damage caused, or alleged to be caused, directly or indirectly by the information contained in this book.

"Things in my life had been going 'OK' before I found Zen's website. I am a therapist and had some problems with a relationship and a few underlying issues as well. I found the intuitive approach gave me the confidence to make choices that I had not been able to make without following my Internal Guidance...it made me think about where the rest of my life was heading...Following your path comes from within and all the money and happiness you could ever wish for will follow as a result. I would strongly recommend this to anyone wishing to further their spiritual path."

Sarah Strudwick—Therapist, United Kingdom

"I have never found anything as life-changing and immediate as this!!! I am witness to profound changes every minute of the day by following your techniques. The 'how to' is so simple and straightforward. It works!"

Elizabeth Crews—Cancer Survivor, Massachusetts

"Zen goes one step farther, she explains in clear detail how to 'feel' your higher self speaking to you and guiding you every step of the way. She calls this your IGS or Internal Guidance System. What amazed me most is that as she tells us how to connect with it, and it was clear to me that it's there and it works!"

Mare—Student, central New York

"I now have control over how my life will go. All my other spiritual work, which I've loved, I see as my path, which brought me to this point right here. More than anything I've ever done I feel I could recommend this to anyone. It's a new way of living your life. There is nothing wrong with being happy. The Internal Guidance System makes me excited. Other spiritual work that I have done I have gotten depressed and stayed in a funk but with the IGS I feel like I have tools to get out of it really quickly."

Gwen W.—Health coordinator, mother, Novato, California

"Her message is very similar to Dr. Wayne Dyer's, but the advantage to Zen's program is she gives us a tool, the IGS, to use in our day-to-day lives in order to get back on track. Other authors in the field are not as clear as to how to self-direct to get yourself back on track. They educate us on what we could or should be doing, Zen directly gives you the how to do it today!"

Lynn W.—non-profit, Rohnert Park, California

*This book is dedicated to my Dad,
Les Kloppenburg,
and dear friend
Bradley Rotter.*

Both have always had unwavering faith in me.

Acknowledgments

My deep appreciation to everyone who has volunteered time and energy to Smart Soul Academy, Ahuma Institute and IGS®, without all of you this work would not be where it is today; the numbers are too many to list. You all know who you are and how much you each mean to me. A very special *yeehaw*, to my best friend, confidant, biggest fan and business partner Kathleen Brucher, for believing in me enough to team up with me to create miracles again and again. My chosen mother Teress Bigio, thank you for your love and support, especially the wonderful way you see me. To Vee Beard and Mary Chase, for getting right away how important the IGS is and dedicating numerous hours to help support its development. Manju Bazzell, thanks for constantly keeping me sane with hours of compassionate conversation, keeping me humble and saying that yes, indeed, I am still on the right track. To the man with the best smile in the world, Lance Freeman, thank you for doing everything that needed to be done with commitment and joy. To Christina Cochrane, that's for your generosity and trusting me. Thank you, Jack Canfield, just having you out there believing in me and the IGS has been a God send, literally. The amazing Smart Soul Team; Tia, Reggie, Shannon, and David for all the enthusiasm and input you are always ready to give. Bradley Rotter, thank you for your loyalty, getting a kick out of all my antics and the twinkle in your eye. My dad, Les Kloppenburg, you have been such a wonderful friend, supporter and have never lost faith in me. Last but never least, to my loving husband, Eric, thanks for ambushing me at just the right moment in my life.

How to Use the Included Instructional Audio CD

The companion CD included with this book is intended to get you started with using your Internal Guidance System® (IGS). It begins with a listening meditation that will help you quickly and easily get into a clearer mental space so that you can more accurately and easily sense your IGS. The next audio track is a simple exercise designed to help you feel your IGS. It is important to practice using the listening meditation at different times throughout the day to build your skill level with it. It is the doorway to using your IGS.

The four exercises on the CD are all there to support you in using your IGS in various situations. Each corresponds to a section in the book. You will find the page numbers that each exercise corresponds to listed on the CD. Start with the first exercise and do it for one week before moving on to the next. Give yourself time to become familiar with each before moving on to the next exercise. This is important because it will allow you to build a deeper understanding of how your IGS works, and will hone your ability to interpret its signals. Once you have used each for a week, either repeat the process of one exercise per week again, or simply use the exercises as you feel you need them.

If you would like to go deeper, do more exercises, and receive mentoring in using your IGS effectively, please go to www.smartsoulacademy.com. There you will find a virtual online training program with coaching and learning partners, and be assigned your very own mentor to ensure you are successful at creating a fulfilling life. We'd be honored to share the journey with you as you learn to use your IGS to create your best life.

Instructional Audio CD

Listening Meditation	Page 24
Feeling the IGS Exercise	Page 26
Noticing Closing Sensations as Guidance	Page 52
Emotions as a Gateway to Your IGS	Page 55
Understanding the Urging of Your IGS	Page 61
Imagining Possibilities	Page 64

Table of Contents

Introduction 13

Section One: What is IGS 19

    What is IGS   21

    How IGS Works   22

    How to Quiet Your Mind to Feel Your IGS   23

    A Simple Exercise to Feel Your IGS   25

    What Did You Feel   27

    Neutral Is One of the Guiding Sensations   28

    Think of Your IGS as a Compass, Not an On/Off Switch   29

    The Anatomy of Your IGS   31

    The IGS Closing Is Always About What *You* Are Thinking   35

    The Source of IGS Guidance   37

The IGS in Relation to Positive and   39
Negative Thoughts

IGS: Always Moving You Toward   41
Fulfillment and Success

Section Two: How to Use Your IGS............ 43

When to Use Your IGS   45

How to Start Using Your IGS Every Day   48

What Was I Thinking   51

Emotions and Your IGS   53

Using Your IGS for Time Management   56

Urging from Your IGS   59

Asking Direct Questions   62

Questions vs. Statements   63

Using Imagination to Receive Guidance from the IGS   64

Four Powerful Questions   65

Is This Any of My Business   66

Is the Thought I Am Having Truthful   67

Is There Anything I Need to Do   69
About This Situation Right Now

Do I Have All the Information I Need to Act   70
Right Now

Section Three: Troubleshooting 71

Asking Too Many Questions · 73

The Frozen Mind: Changing the Channel · 75

Pushing to Change the Response from Your IGS · 77

Not Trusting the Neutral · 79

Compulsively Reversing Questions When in Doubt · 80

Closing Is Just Closing · 82

Don't Panic if You Followed the Closing · 84

Keep in Motion · 86

The IGS Rarely Leads You Directly from Point A to Point B · 87

You Cannot Trick Your IGS · 89

Section Four: Conclusion 91

"Be the Change You Wish to See in the World" · 93

Every Day Sacred · 94

Every Day Sacred Does Not Equal "Every Day Perfect" · 96

Enjoying the Process · 97

Introduction

Introduction

In the mid-90s I stumbled across the term Internal Guidance System. A little-known couple named the Hicks was touring the U.S. in their motor home teaching people about the Law of Attraction. Someone gave me a cassette recording of one of the lectures, and I remember being intrigued by the material and was quite affected by their explanation of what they then called the Internal Guidance System. I knew that I felt in my own body what they were describing. In fact, I had been feeling it all my life.

Although the Hicks talked about the Internal Guidance System® and what it felt like, they did not give any concrete teachings on how it works or how to follow it. I began to try to find other books or material on Internal Guidance, Inner Guidance, or anything resembling the sensations I felt. I could not find anything except tiny references that it exists—certainly nothing that could teach me how to actually use or even understand it. That is where my passion to discover everything about my Internal Guidance System ignited.

The idea that the sensations I felt were actually guidance from some deeper, wiser part of myself was an exciting and inspiring thought to me. Over the next few years I experimented over and over on own guidance system. I became skilled at how the guidance worked, I discovered what got in the way of my listening to it, and finally recognized and valued what would happen if I made a commitment to only follow the guidance I received. What I found was astonishing. This little guidance system had great power in leading me toward feeling fulfilled and recognizing how I was able to attain success in every area of my life. There was nothing that I could not rely on for this guidance system to help me with. It was able to untangle all the messes I got myself into and open up doors I never dreamed were possible.

By 2001 I was a CEO of a boutique Internet design firm in San Francisco, California. It was just as the dot-com boom was ending and the first market crash had occurred. The firm we had started was not a part of the dot-com explosion but rather working with Fortune 500 firms with solid capital and stability. However, the stability of our clients did not matter. The second crash was felt around the world, and soon my partners and I found ourselves in 1.2 million dollars of personally secured debt. I had followed my Internal Guidance System, which by now I referred to as my IGS®, into this amazing industry, building a solid company, with a great team. Now it was time to follow my IGS out of the situation to see how it was able to steward us when in times of deep fear and pain.

That is exactly what I did. My IGS kept me sane and was able to even keep me feeling happy and confident during one of the most trying periods of my life. In fact, I was so unusually calm and happy that my friends, who were also experiencing the pain of the crash, began to ask me to either give them the name of the drugs I was taking or tell them my secret. So I told them my secret, and from that moment on I began to share and teach others about their IGS. The years of gained knowledge of how the IGS operates, how to interpret its guidance, and most importantly how to remove all the obstacles our mind, the world, and our ego puts in the way of following this guidance, were poured into those who were looking for help.

My IGS completely transformed the way I experienced my past and my present, and created my vision of the future. I found that when I mulled over old hurts from my childhood, whether it be family or friends that had caused the pain, I could sense what was the actual truth of the situations—how I remembered them and what had happened from all perspectives involved. My IGS was able to help me leave the pain and scarring behind forever. In listening to my IGS, my relationships transformed, including healing my relationship with my father, I was able to enjoy my brother as I watched him get deathly sick and pass away, and it gave me compassion for the children who teased me mercilessly in school when I was growing up.

All the ways that the painful situations in my life had left their mark began to be erased, bringing me closer and closer to who I truly am inside. I was able to show the world my beauty and truth. It gave me the courage to set boundaries, speak my truth, and admit when I was wrong. The doubt I felt about what I should do in life

Introduction

went away. I suddenly understood clearly in the moment how to communicate my needs and how to listen to the needs of others. There was this beautiful sensation of being comfortable in my own skin, and I gained a love and appreciation for myself, even when I considered myself not perfect.

In my love relationships it brought me out of the destructive and painful patterns I was repeating over and over again—the same old stuff, just a different man. I was able to understand what part I played in the ongoing relationship sagas. All the ways of talking negatively to my partners, and my attempts to manipulate and control them to get what I wanted, were now revealed. The amazing thing is that, when these negative aspects of my actions were revealed, it was not painful, but a relief! When your IGS shows you your faults or the ugly things about yourself you don't even want to see, it does so in such a way that you feel wonderful and empowered.

My IGS is able to support me in following my dreams, just in the way it naturally operates, allowing me to hang tough when things don't look like they are going to work out, or to know when to stop moving down an unfruitful path. I have never had so much joy and success in my life as when I began to follow the nudgings of my IGS. What amazed me most is how it knows all the things it does, just how accurate it is, and how precisely it informs and guides me. I have received guidance not to take a business trip only to find out that the event was cancelled a week after I was going to pay for my travel arrangements. Every day I pick up the phone and hear the person say, "Amazing! I was just thinking about you this very moment." I have cancelled plans and found out that the friend I was supposed to meet really needed to be home with a sick child, feeling ever so grateful that I was the one to do the cancelling.

My IGS manages my time and the sequence of how things get accomplished in my life. It controls what I call the flow—how my life literally flows along. Day after day I get so much done it is mind-boggling. I have what I need just as I need it or just before I need it. When the time is not right for something to be done, I can feel my IGS guiding me away from starting the task. This alone has saved me thousands of dollars and countless hours of wasted effort. I see this as one of the most powerful unexplored business tools on the planet.

People often ask me why so many seemingly magical, synergistic things happen to me in my life. My answer is that the real way the world works is when we get out of our own way, when we stop trying to force things, and when we follow this wise little system called IGS. Now I am not alone in all these discoveries. There are thousands of people using their IGS every day, getting the same results and feeling tremendous gratitude for this new way of living. Everyone has their very own IGS. It is looking out for you just as it is for me. So begin your journey knowing that you will start seeing magical synergy in your life as this remarkable, natural, and innate guidance brings you ultimate fulfillment and success. The best news is you already have it; it is turned on and already working. Now, all you need to do is tap into it and start your own flow of life.

~Zen DeBrücke

What Is IGS

Section One

What Is IGS

You were born with a factory-installed guidance system. It is like the GPS in a car. Its purpose is to get you from one end of your life to the other with the most joy, ease, and fulfillment possible. It knows everything that you desire and how you most yearn for those things to be accomplished. This factory-installed system is called Internal Guidance System or IGS, for those in the know.

> *"The purpose of our life is happiness."*
>
> ~ Dali Lama

Your IGS is very much like a wise best friend who is constantly there to support you, give you guidance, and enjoy your life with you all along the way. In fact, your IGS is so amazing and interesting that I had to write an entire book to introduce you to it.

How IGS Works

Your IGS provides guidance by giving you sensations in your body. It resides in the area between your throat and solar plexus (the area that is the triangle where your ribs come together, above your stomach). The sensations that you feel in this area of your body are forms of guidance.

Your IGS guides you in two distinct ways.

1. It creates sensations that correspond to your thoughts. No matter when or where you are, as you are thinking, your IGS is listening and helping to guide your mind toward greater ease and fulfillment in that moment.

2. Your IGS creates what I like to call a nudging feeling. It nudges you to move toward various activities in the world around you. As an example, think of the last time you had a nudging to call a friend. When you followed that nudging, did your friend respond with "I was just thinking of you!" or possibly "I really needed to talk to you. How did you know?"

> *"The most wonderful aspect of the universal scheme of things is the action of free beings under divine guidance."*
>
> ~Joseph Marie de Maistre

Both of these forms of guidance combine to provide you with information that supports you to:

1. Respond to your life as it develops.
2. Encourage you to create your future, as you desire it to be.

By learning to follow your IGS, you will find that all of life seems to work out, being just perfect in the way it unfolds, and you become a magnet for small or large miracles.

How to Quiet Your Mind to Feel Your IGS

First, it is important to get yourself relaxed, centered, and grounded. Sit up straight with both feet on the floor. With your eyes closed allow yourself to move from head to toe, slowly relaxing every part of your body as your awareness moves downward from your head to your torso, down into your legs, to your feet. Then feel the feeling in your feet as they rest on the floor. Relax, breathe deeply, and feel the force of gravity gently helping you to sink more deeply into your chair.

Now, shift your awareness to your chest and to your breath. Notice what it feels like to breathe, to expand your chest, and then to let it relax. Take a few deep breaths, and let yourself make a sound as you exhale if that helps you to release tension. Feel the muscles in the chest area and notice any tension there. Next, become aware of your neck, shoulders, and upper back. If you feel tense or tight in these areas, move your shoulders and neck around so you can release the tension. Remain aware of your breathing.

> *"When we need to find God, he cannot be found in the noise and restlessness. God is the friend of silence. See how nature—trees, flowers, grass—grows in silence; see the stars, the moon and the sun, how they move in silence.... We need silence to be able to touch our souls."*
>
> ~Mother Teresa

While focusing on your feet as they rest on the floor, begin to pay attention to what you are hearing around you. Bringing awareness to what you are hearing as you feel your feet helps you to release the thoughts your mind is generating and relax more deeply into this process. It may take a few minutes if you are not used to relaxing the mind by focusing on two aspects in particular; let yourself take the time you need to really listen, allowing the release of your mind from thinking. As you focus on hearing, try not to judge or name what you are hearing; instead, just experience the sounds. If you find at any time during the exercise your mind gets active again, just relax and notice your feet on the floor and go back to listening to what is both near and far away.

Please refer to the corresponding
exercise on the audio CD.

A Simple Exercise to Feel Your IGS

When you are relaxed and noticing sounds, bring your awareness into your chest, keeping your eyes closed. Then, let the statement below pass quietly, slowly, and repeatedly if necessary through your mind. Try not to hold on to the thought or concentrate on it, and instead simply see the statement floating through your mind as if it were a cloud passing through the sky. If your mind has a reaction to the statement, just let that thought go and put your focus back on what you are hearing. You might want to repeat it again out loud. When you think or say the thought to yourself, notice the very first sensation you feel in the area between your throat and stomach area. If you feel something, describe it to yourself in words or write it down on a piece of paper.

> *"What lies behind you and what lies in front of you, pales in comparison to what lies inside of you."*
>
> ~ Ralph Waldo Emerson

Here is the statement:

*I **do not** have an Internal Guidance System.*

When you've noted your sensation, then move on and try the statement below in the same way. Notice what you are hearing without naming or judging the sounds. Relax, keep your eyes closed, and, when your mind quiets, see the following thought as a cloud passing through the sky of your mind:

*I **do** have an Internal Guidance System.*

Again, notice the very first sensation you feel between your chest and stomach area. Describe it to yourself in words or write out the sensations you feel. It could be a strong feeling or a very subtle one. If you have no sensation at all, don't be concerned. This is a very normal response when first becoming aware of your IGS. Focus again on the feeling of your lungs filling with air, putting all your attention on the sensation of listening, and try one more time before moving on.

If you had trouble or did not notice anything, you can listen to an audio meditation on our website. It may be easier to just relax and let me guide you through the process. Go to www.smartsoulacademy.com/IGSmeditation and do the meditation there.

Please refer to the corresponding
exercise on the audio CD.

What Did You Feel?

What you may have felt in this exercise are sensations of expansion/opening and contraction/closing in your chest area.

When you stated *I do not have an Internal Guidance System*, you may have felt a tightening, a constriction, or pressure in your chest area. For some, it feels like a "dropping" or a "wilting." Others realize it is the familiar feeling of anxiety, stress, or worry. This is the sensation I will refer to as "closing" or "closed" throughout the book.

When you stated *I do have an Internal Guidance System*, you may have noticed that your chest area seemed to "open up." Some describe it as an expansion, a release of pressure, a relaxing feeling, and an upward opening of energy rising in a V or Y shape or a sense of lightness. This is what I refer to as "opening" or "open" throughout the book. If you felt none of these things, don't worry. It is there, and you will begin to realize what it is as you explore further.

> *"Happiness is a continuation of happenings which are not resisted."*
>
> ~ Deepak Chopra

Some people live in their minds strategizing, planning, and creating. If this is true for you, you may be so used to not feeling the sensations in your body that you want to spend a bit more time focusing on feeling the body before you recognize the sensations of your IGS. The exercises in this book will support you in connecting your IGS to your thoughts naturally. So just read on and, in no time, you will be delighted to discover you are easily feeling and receiving the insightful guidance of your IGS.

Neutral Is One of the Guiding Sensations

Not feeling anything may simply be guidance being given as a "neutral sensation," which is still information from your IGS. The IGS generates three types of sensations in varying degrees: opening, closing, *and* neutral. It is important to remember that each sensation can carry a different level of intensity.

Often people have trouble feeling IGS sensations because of a preconceived notion of what the experience should feel like. The mind looks for what it thinks the IGS is going to feel like, instead of what you are actually feeling. The solution to this is to focus on your feet and to listen to the sounds around you, both far and near. Keep relaxing into the feeling and the sounds, and then make the statements. Repeat the statement several times, silently or out loud, while relaxing. Instead of *trying* to feel the sensations of your IGS, just let it just happen by putting your awareness and mind on the sentence.

> *"Every time you don't follow your inner guidance, you feel a loss of energy, loss of power, a sense of spiritual deadness."*
>
> ~ Shakti Gawain

In addition, our minds are so active and powerful that it can be difficult to isolate one thought for this exercise. Your mind may be trying to focus on the statements in the exercise but your actual thoughts are, "Is that it? What does that mean? I do not have an Internal Guidance System. Of course I have a guidance system. Am I still feeling my feet?" This is not focusing on one thought, and your IGS responds to all thoughts. It can take practice, but as you read on further there will be lots of ways given to begin recognizing the sensations of your IGS.

Think of Your IGS as a Compass, Not an On/Off Switch

One of the first conclusions that people come to is that the IGS operates as a *yes* or a *no*. They assume that if you feel closed that is a no, and if you feel open you are getting a yes. This is not how it operates. Your IGS is closer to a compass that is used to navigate the planet.

A compass, when guiding you toward north, is always moving slightly back and forth. This is due to the fact that true magnetic north fluctuates and is not fixed. Your IGS is always fluctuating, too: opening and closing, always slightly shifting as what you are thinking shifts and changes. It is very attuned to where the focus of your thoughts is leading you.

If you picture only half of a compass, for our example, north is your greatest joy, west is neutral, and south is your most terrifying sensations of panic and despair. Your IGS will give you sensations from one end of the spectrum to the other, all based on whether your thoughts are moving you forward into a fulfilled life or away from it. Think of your IGS as the needle on the compass, which has many different points: south—panic, southwest—anxiety, west—calm, northwest—happy and peaceful, north—joy. Of course there are many differing sensations from the south point to the north point, and each is giving you the degree of fulfillment or lack of fulfillment you are moving toward.

It is important to note that these are not emotions but what the sensations often feel like when they are experienced. Later we will discuss the difference between emotional energy and the sensations your IGS gives you.

Another way to think about the guidance from your IGS is similar to the hot or cold game we played as children where one child is blindfolded and the others try to guide the blindfolded child toward the prize using the terms *colder, cold, warm, warmer, hot,* and *hottest.* This is exactly how your IGS works in guiding you, except it uses varying levels of opening, neutral, and closing sensations! The more expanded, opening energy you feel, the more your thoughts are moving you in a successful direction, and the more you feel closed sensations like worry, fear, stress, and panic, the farther your thoughts are carrying you away from having success.

The Anatomy of Your IGS

Your IGS has three areas where sensations can occur as guidance: throat, chest and stomach. When you feel sensations in these areas, you are having thoughts that fall into three categories: 1) Dis-empowering yourself personally, 2) Real-time information regarding thoughts you are having about actions to take or have taken, and 3) Beliefs that you have that are keeping you away from moving toward success and fulfillment.

Throat

Have you ever felt a tightening or a closing in your throat? It can almost feel like you have something lodged in your throat or possibly like you cannot swallow? This is guidance from your IGS. It means the thoughts you are having about yourself are limiting you from what are truly capable of, or are not empowering you toward achieving success in the situation you are in. Very often the emotion of shame or embarrassment accompanies the closing. The throat area does not have the opening sensation that the chest does. It is open most of the time except when the thoughts mentioned above are present.

> *"God, to me, it seems, is a verb, not a noun, proper or improper."*
>
> ~ Richard Buckminster Fuller

Examples of such thoughts are:

He/she really doesn't love me, understand me, or care about me.

I have failed again. I will never get ahead in life, this job, or this relationship.

I can't say what I really feel, think, or believe. I will be hurt, rejected, or attacked.

I sound stupid, ridiculous, embarrassed, or ignorant.

If you feel a closing in your throat area, check the thoughts your mind is creating about who you are being or how you think you are being perceived by others in the situation. When you find the thoughts you will find they are about your not having power. Your IGS is letting you know these thoughts are *not true, this is not how others are perceiving you,* and they are not guiding you toward fulfillment and success. I will provide exercises in Section Two that help in shifting to opening thoughts.

Chest

When your chest is experiencing the opening sensation, it can feel as slight as a hint of relaxation or as strong as a rush of expanding energy, depending on how on target toward fulfillment are your thoughts. When your chest is experiencing the closing sensation, it can feel slightly tight or it can feel like a panic attack, depending on how far away the thoughts are taking you from being fulfilled.

The sensations of the chest are in relation to what you are thinking about the immediate past, current moment, or future. This area of the IGS is what is most commonly felt on a regular basis and provides the most effective guidance throughout your normal day. Examples of these thoughts are:

> I should do the grocery shopping after work today. (open/closed)

> My new client seems to be wavering; maybe I should offer them something as an incentive. (open/closed)

> I have not heard back from my friend regarding attending our party. Did I do something to upset him/her? (open/closed)

Sensations in your chest are giving you guidance on everyday living. By going about your life, if you stay aware of this area of your body, it will guide you toward being more at ease and in the flow. I have provided exercises in Section Two that will begin to help you build your awareness and understand this type of guidance.

Solar Plexus

The guidance you receive from this area of your IGS is life-changing. The sensations in this area, the solar plexus, when closed feel like an upset stomach, as if there is a rock, or a churning tightness. You will find that it is constant; it does not expand and contract like your chest area does. As you move about your day, no matter what you are thinking, doing, or feeling, it is still there. It does not come and go but just stays and can become the background sensation that you may or may not be aware of unless you slow down. There is not a corresponding opening sensation in this area. If you are open in this area you will not notice at all.

The importance of this area is that it is informing you of a belief system or what I refer to as a body of thought. This is when you have one large, all-informing idea about yourself, your life, or how the world works that is not true. This belief/body of thought is keeping you from the true perspective, which will lead you to success.

Examples of this:

> I am unlovable, unattractive, broken, or a failure.
>
> I will never get ahead in life, be successful, or have what I dream of.
>
> Life is against me, is painful, or is too hard.
>
> I have no one to support me, I cannot get a break, or things always go wrong.

These may not seem like thoughts that you hold. I have broken them down to their simplest form. What they look like when you hold them while in your relationship, as an example, is that your partner can never tell you that he or she loves you enough. Everything that he/she does is attributed to not loving you or being supportive enough of you. When this happens your mind brings to the forefront all kinds of past and present situations that it uses to prove that this belief/body of thought is accurate. Your solar plexus closes and stays that way as long as you are generating the story. There's more on how to shift this in Section Two.

Another aspect of the solar plexus is if you have a life-changing event occur: losing your job, a divorce, or some situation that can dramatically affect your future. All of your thoughts begin to revolve around the new projected future. For example, you lose your job, and then all of your thoughts become about how much money you have to survive on, what you are no longer able to afford, or fears of how you are going to keep up the lifestyle you are accustomed to. You may find yourself turning down offers to do things with friends, worrying in the grocery store about the cheapest items, or cutting out things that are not necessarily what you should be sacrificing.

> *"In Zen Buddhism, Satori is a moment of Presence, a brief stepping out of the voice in your head, the thought processes, and their reflection in the body as emotion. It is the arising of inner spaciousness where before there was the clutter of thought and the turmoil of emotion."*
>
> ~Eckhart Tolle, A New Earth: Awakening to Your Life's Purpose

You may find that that this overwhelming body of thought takes over every aspect of your life. This is when your IGS will send guidance in the form of a closing in your solar plexus so that you can become aware of how these thoughts are not bringing you toward greater fulfillment and are quite possibly creating what you do not want more of in your life. If cutting costs and being aware of the possible savings are in order, you will feel empowered and open as you make these choices. Your IGS will always provide you with a sense of ease and satisfaction when what you are choosing is truly leading you toward more success in any situation.

The IGS Closing Is Always About What *You* Are Thinking

When I first began my attempt to understand the sensations from my IGS, I found that the most challenging thing to remember is that the guidance was only about what I was thinking. When I opened, it was about the thoughts I was having, and when I closed, it was about the thoughts I was having. This dramatic shift—from the belief that others and the world around us—is attributed to what is making us feel bad or good. It can take constantly reminding yourself to change how you are thinking about something or someone.

Every person I have ever taught how to use his or her IGS has begun the process with this backward in his/her mind. When he/she feels closing (i.e., anxiety, worry, or fear), he/she believes that something bad is going to happen, that the person he/she is thinking about is the problem, or that what he/she is thinking is going to come true. This is *false*! The way it works is when you get a closing sensation, that means what you are thinking is not going to happen, is not the truth, is not accurate, and it is not leading you toward success.

Let's say you get a phone call from a client, they are rushed and they cancel an appointment with you. You begin to think maybe they are unhappy with your work or product. Possibly your mind brings up fears you have about your work or product and then attributes this to the action your client just took. Most often in these situations you will get a corresponding sensation of tightness in your IGS. Let's say it is in your solar plexus. All of our life we have had these feelings and since we actually physically feel what we perceive as uncomfortable sensations (IGS guidance), we assume that it is because the client is unhappy with us, and there is a part of us that *knows* this. When working with your IGS the most challenging aspect in the beginning is to remember that the closing means your thoughts are not true and they are leading you *away* from fulfillment and success. What if you continue down the thought path that your client is unhappy? What would you do? Call them and try to fix the situation? Find out what is wrong? Second-guess them and try to solve a problem that you have made up? You can quickly see how this can lead to a chain reaction that at its least is a waste of energy and at its most will damage or cause you to lose the relationship with your client.

Now if you stop when you sense the closing sensation, feel your body, quiet your mind, and observe what you are thinking, you'll recognize that your IGS is letting you know the thoughts are not true and leading you away from success with your client. You can then begin focusing on finding the thoughts that open you, leading you toward what is more true and what are more fulfilling, successful thoughts. In the beginning simply reverse the thoughts you are having and see if this begins the opening.

As you read further it is important to remember that closing sensations only occur when your thoughts are not true and are moving you away from success. If you are experiencing closing sensations (bad feeling in the area of your IGS, uneasiness, fear, anxiety, worry, or concern) about someone or something, that means what you are thinking is not true or needs to be reexamined to find what perspective opens you. If there is a problem, or when you are thinking about a problem, your IGS will give you an opening sensation, meaning what you are thinking is true and something you need to focus on solving.

The Source of IGS Guidance

This is one of the most interesting aspects of your IGS. To be frank, I cannot be completely sure myself. What I do know from all my years of experience is that the guidance is very wise, seems to know everything that needs to be taken into account in the situation, *and* works out perfectly for everyone involved. These facts alone are still astounding to me, even though I am used to it by now. When you begin to follow your IGS you quickly begin to realize that it knows things about the past, present, and future that your mind could not possibly know. Your IGS understands more about you and your limiting beliefs/thoughts than are you are able to understand about yourself.

What I suggest is that you explore your IGS and then decide for yourself where you feel it gets its guidance from. I can speak for myself that what opens me when I ponder on this topic is that my IGS is a broader, wiser, and more infinite part of me: my higher Self, Divine Self, the Holy Spirit. It is referenced in many wisdom traditions from indigenous tribes to world religions. It is the energy that is running through all of life and is engaged in all aspects of our Universe. It operates out of space and time so it can see where your thoughts are leading you and what the ramifications are going to be if you continue on a path of thought. Guidance is given on every aspect of your life—not just the big things, but the little things, too.

I remember one instance where I got out of a business meeting early. On my way home I thought I would stop by the grocery store and do my shopping so I would not have to leave the house again later. (I love missing the rush hour at the grocery store.) As I was thinking about which store to go to and what I would purchase, I realized my chest was tight, and I was feeling stressed, which is my IGS closing. I thought, "That is strange." Over the years I have learned not to try to figure out why I am opened or closed, and that, when I simply trust this guidance, things work out so much better. I thought, "Well, I guess I had better head home," and my chest area began to relax, which is the opening of my IGS.

As I pulled on to my street I saw the cable repair truck in front of our home. The repairman was just picking up the orange cones and putting them in the back of his van. I rolled down my window and asked if he was there for our house. He said yes. He had gotten a report that our DVR was not working. This was a very big deal! My roommate was a basketball fan—a big basketball fan—and it was March Madness. He was missing it while he was at work. He had made the appointment and forgot. I let the repairman in, he fixed it, and all was well with the world. You cannot imagine how happy my roommate was that I just *happened* to be there.

> *"The mind can assert anything and pretend it has proved it. My beliefs I test on my body, on my intuitional consciousness, and when I get a response there, then I accept."*
>
> ~ D.H. Lawrence

You will come to your own conclusions about where the IGS gets its information, or maybe you will decide to just let it be a mystery. Over time coincidence, synchronicity, miracles, and just plain ol' luck will become common. You hit the post office, bank, grocery store, you name it, while there is no line. Or five minutes later tons of people walk in and you are already on your way out. In fact, by following your IGS this will become so common that you will be shocked when something happens that is not that way—which generally means you have not been paying attention to your IGS, and it is time to get back on track.

The IGS in Relation to Positive and Negative Thoughts

People often believe that it is simply a matter of having positive or negative thoughts—that the IGS is opening and closing based on the quality of their thoughts. This is actually not the case. Your IGS can open when you are feeling emotionally upset, and it can close when you are feeling emotionally happy. The emotions you have are not the same as your IGS. Your emotions are separate and distinct from your IGS. Feeling hopeful has led many people into situations that were not the best for them—and vice versa: feeling emotionally distraught has created wreckage in what otherwise were good situations.

Your IGS leads you regardless of how you are feeling. You can attempt to hold positive thoughts in a situation that is not going to bring you fulfillment and success, and, no matter how much you hope that it will, your IGS will not open. As you learn to use your IGS over time you will discover how this aspect of your IGS works.

One student of Smart Soul Academy learned this in a very striking way. She recounts her experience:

"I am in training to be a yoga teacher. It is my passion and I wanted all of my family to experience the joy of yoga. For a while I had been attempting to get my cousin to go to a yoga class with me. One day out of the blue she called me to say she wanted to go with me and in fact could make the ten o'clock class that day. I was so overjoyed! We made a plan to meet at the yoga studio. As I was getting ready to go I realized I was feeling closed; this was quite a surprise, for I really wanted to attend the class with her. Knowing better than to second-guess my IGS I called her back and told her that my IGS was closed. She said that was fine we could attend the one o'clock class instead.

"When the time came I jumped in my car and was heading over to meet her. All the way there I was feeling a closing sensation again! So I called her on the phone, suggested she go without me, and headed back home. Within a short while I got a call from my daughter's school. She was very sick, and I needed to pick her up immediately. If I had been in class I would have missed the call from the school. What is most amazing to me was realizing that I could feel excited and happy but get a closing feeling. It really made it clear that I need to pay attention to my IGS no matter how I am feeling."

This is just one example. Now let's look at how it can be the other way when you are feeling unpleasant and get an opening. Another student had this experience:

"My week had been really challenging. Long hours at work and I was feeling rundown physically, which made everything more difficult. I had made a commitment to go to a friend's art event that Thursday evening. When I was leaving work I was thinking of all the reasons why I should stay home and rest. As I had these thoughts I realized I was closed. This was very strange to me since I really did not want to go; I was tired and just wanted to sit on the couch and watch TV. I did not want to get dressed and go out at all. When I changed my thoughts to I really should just push myself and go, I opened.

"What was so funny is I spent the next hour arguing with my IGS. It is so strange when you get to the place where you are arguing with what your IGS is telling you. Yet every time I thought of going, no matter how grumpy I was about it, I still opened. So I went. I had a great time; I laughed, met great new people, and felt completely refreshed the next day. Needless to say my IGS knew better than I did what was best for me. What I really needed after all was some fun."

Be aware of your IGS as you experience your emotions. They are often based on what your mind thinks is the truth, which is not necessarily what will bring you the most fulfillment and success.

IGS: Always Moving You Toward Fulfillment and Success

Your IGS is always guiding you toward what is best for you *and* best for everyone around you. This may seem like too large of a task to be possible for your own little IGS, however, let me assure that it is the absolute truth.

What I have come to realize is everyone in my life is there for a purpose. Everyone whose life I am apart of, I am a part of it for a purpose. If there is no purpose in the connection, we just seem to fade away, or we conflict in some way that has us not contact one another or we never really stick to begin with. You know what I mean—like when you meet someone you think is just great but then never contact him/her or possibly never see him/her after that. This is what I mean by having a purpose in each other's lives.

The guidance your IGS is giving you is specific for your life. It takes into account how you are to think, feel and behave in order for you to be fulfilled and successful in every situation you encounter. If there is a difficult situation or conversation that you need to have it will lead you to the most fulfilling and successful conclusion for you and everyone concerned. Now let me be clear: It may not seem that way when the moment is occurring. Yet if you follow your IGS in thought and speech, you will find that this is absolutely the outcome that occurs.

"If you don't like something change it; if you can't change it, change the way you think about it."

~ Mary Engelbreit

One of my clients was trying to make a very difficult decision. She had a job opportunity 1,500 miles away from where she lived. The difficulty was that her husband, who loved his job, did not want to move. Their children were happy where they were living. They were both thriving at school and had a community of friends that were important to them. Yet what opened her was taking the new position.

They went over and over the decision, together. Her husband had an opening in his IGS about her going, but he could not get over being left to raise their children alone most of the time. They both had lots of thought about how hard it would be, and how they would be lonely, and they feared this would cause an end to their marriage. All of these thoughts closed both of them, meaning that they were not true, and the thoughts of hardship were actually not moving them into the direction of success.

In the end they decided to follow their openings, and she took the position. They all got along fine and their marriage actually blossomed! They had to be very clear and aligned about decisions with the children; they planned beautiful, fun weekends when she came home (which they had never made time to do before); and the two of them found ways to be more connected and romantic together. A new passion for each other was the result of their realizing how much they truly meant to each other.

She stayed in the position for six months, and then out of nowhere was offered another wonderful position in the area from which she had just come. It opened them both for her to take that position. They cite those six months as what bought their relationship back to life, united their family, and gave them a new way of prioritizing their relationship, and it continues to be a gift to this day.

How to Use Your IGS

Section Two

When to Use Your IGS

The best time to use your IGS is *always*! It does not do you any good to use it only when you are confused, don't know what to do, or are so closed that you feel horrible. The best way to incorporate it into your life is as you are going about your day. Of course it takes practice to remember to feel the sensations, but this quickly turns into a habit. The wonderful thing about your IGS is that you can *feel* it; it is able to wake you up when you are flowing toward something you don't desire.

Picture yourself going about your day and in the background you are worried about how your child is doing in school. Perhaps you have been called into a parent teacher conference and your mind is running every scenario possible about what his/her teacher is going to discuss with you. Not only that, but your mind is also beating you up for ever parenting "mistake" you believe you have made recently.

Suddenly, you realize you have a rock in your solar plexus, and your chest is tight, and you are filled with anxiety. You have started practicing using your IGS and realize that you have a belief/body of thought that is *not true and not leading you toward fulfillment and success!* As you examine what you were thinking, you realize that all of your thoughts were of getting in trouble for the way your child is acting in school, and that you were thinking thoughts that brought on emotions like shame, embarrassment, and failure. However these beliefs, you realize, are not true, for you are receiving a closing sensation.

Your chest is closed, so you realize that the meeting in your near future is not going to go the way it is being played out in your head. So you focus on finding a new perspective and look for what is opening you.

Everyone's kids have their issues. Mine are no worse than anyone else's. This a normal way to feel as a parent.

Everyone feels like his or her parenting style can use some work.

The teacher is there to help me, and we are on the same team.

> *"From a somatic perspective, Spirit is a felt bodily state. It's an embodiment of a state of consciousness in which the attributes of depth, connection, power, being, unity, wholeness, and love are directly experienced. It's a process, not an end state, in which one is moved and informed by a power called energy, ki, chi, élan vital, prana, shabd, (holy spirit) depending on the language of your culture. This energy is experienced as larger than the self, yet includes it and is accompanied by humility and awe at the mystery of life. When the body is touched by the energy of Spirit, the "I" we normally think of as our self no longer holds center stage; thus the heightened experience of depth and connection has a more universal feeling about it, even though we are more personally present and intimate with the world. Life if filled with more order and meaning, even though the normal "me" is not making meaning and order.*
>
> *The embodied experience of Spirit ties our common sense in knots—we're in choice, but out of control; disorganized, but stable; still while in movement; knowing without understanding; listening without ears; surrendering to be victorious; giving in to succeed; dying to live. This paradox of embodied Spirit is often described in terms of grace, awe, unity, reverence, presence, wonder and beauty."*
>
> ~Richard Strozzi-Heckler, The Leadership Dojo

As you hold these thoughts you begin to feel ease in your solar plexus and your chest, which of course lets you know that these thought are closer to reality than the previous thoughts. You are able to focus on work, you feel better, and you even feel a good expectation that the meeting is going to go well.

This type of moment is the gold produced by using your IGS all the time. By not putting it on a shelf and taking it down when you are in trouble or confusion, you clean out the anxiety-ridden thoughts your mind produces. Pay attention to your body, and to the sensations in the area of your IGS. That way, you can keep your energy feeling open and creative. Looking at the scenario above, can you imagine how you would feel more flexible, creative, and open when walking into the meeting with the new opening perspectives? Be aware of your IGS throughout your day.

How to Start Using Your IGS Every Day

Bringing awareness to your IGS can take time and focus. The IGS has been with you since you were born; yet no one knew to teach you what the sensations meant. What often happens for most people, since they did not know that the opening and closing actually meant something, is that they begin to ignore the feelings. Another way that the sensations were dealt with is that their mind began to assign meaning to the opening and closing—i.e., when feeling pressure in the chest, that meant the person talking was intending on hurting me. Both of these responses lead to challenges in reconnecting with your IGS as daily guidance.

In the first situation people have trouble recognizing the sensations at all. The resulting effect is living completely within the mind, in strategy, logic, and the imagination. In the second situation the person can find him/herself triggered or overly emotional to the encounters he/she finds him/herself in.

The way to know if you are one or the other (or possibly you switch back and forth between the two) is to look at how your daily life unfolds. If you find that your day zips by and you lose part of your day, where you don't remember it, you could be person number one. Some of you might be thinking, "What? How can you lose part of your day?" Have you ever driven home and could not remember the drive home? Have you ever been flowing right along in a project and looked up to find that it is four o'clock in the afternoon, yet the last time you looked at the clock it was ten o'clock in the morning? This is classic for those who are spending their time living within their minds. There is nothing wrong with this at all—it is one way of living—but learning to be aware of your body and your IGS has unique challenges.

To analyze if you are in the second situation, you will look at how much of your day is spent in an emotional state. Do you get upset by something that happens and lose all of your focus? Instead of being able to continue on with your day, your mind keeps interrupting your focus in many ways: by rerunning the offensive encounter, arguing with the person, coming up with all the reasons why he/she is wrong or has no right to treat you that way, or projecting into the future how things are going to go end up in painful resolutions.

I am one who does both of these things. If you are the first type, then what is important is to begin by bringing your awareness to your body throughout the day. The quieting your mind exercise in the beginning of this book is a wonderful way to start. Start by feeling your feet, being aware of your breath, and listen to the sounds in the area around you. We have a body awareness practice that you can do throughout the day without anyone knowing you're doing it. You can listen to it or download it for free at www.smartsoulacademy.com/setpoint.

As you remember to focus on your body, you will find that each time you check in, an IGS sensation can be felt. Remember there are openings, closings, and neutrals. So even if you just feel neutral, you are feeling your IGS. Once you are feeling your IGS sensations more often, move on to the next practice below.

If you are a person whose mind has attached emotions to the sensations of your IGS, it will still be important to quiet yourself and feel your body. Often in emotional experiences we may feel a great deal; however, we are feeling our emotional energy and not grounded in our bodies. So start by feeling your feet, being aware of your breath, and listen to the sounds in the area around you. Next notice the sensation of your IGS. Don't assume that it will be closed. I have often been more surprised when I was in the emotions of hurt, anger, or frustration only to realize I was open and that these feelings were authentic and experiencing them actually helped me move toward fulfillment and success.

When connecting to your body, begin feeling your IGS discover the guidance under the emotional energy. Are you open or are you closed? If you are open, stay with the emotion but be aware of your thoughts. Very often, if you just realize that your thoughts are true and in alignment, a calmness of being, if not a calming of your emotions, begins to occur.

However, if you realize you are closed, then this is what you do. State to yourself:

I am closed. That means that what I am thinking is not true and not bringing me toward fulfillment and success.

This is one of the most powerful beginning practices that will quickly get you in touch with your IGS. Since your IGS is always giving you guidance on what you are thinking, this thought being true, will ever so slightly begin to open you each time you focus upon it.

You will begin to feel that opening and gain confidence that you are really feeling it, and that what you are thinking really is not true or bringing you fulfillment. Stay with that thought over and over. Feel the closing again; make the statement; feel the opening begin. I have found that this one statement builds awareness, trust, and connection with the IGS more than anything else.

What Was I Thinking

The next step in developing your awareness of your IGS is becoming aware of what you are thinking. Since your IGS is giving you guidance on your thoughts, then it is important to realize what your thoughts are made of. This may seem like a very simple endeavor, but surprisingly it is quite challenging. Most people find that they are cruising along in life and suddenly realize that they are closed. When they then go to find the closing thoughts, they cannot remember what they were thinking! Do not think you are crazy or alone. This still happens to me on occasion. We are not used to paying close attention to what our mind is really doing as we are living our lives.

At first the most important element is to realize when you are closed. Why not open, you might ask? Well, when we are feeling pleasant and good, we have a tendency to just keep moving right along. It is when we feel unpleasant that we wake up and pay attention. The closing is our alarm bell—our wake-up call. Since it is an alarm bell, it is often easier to remember to pay attention to the guidance our IGS is giving. The openings will become more and more important as you gain conscious access to your IGS.

You may find at first that you cannot remember what your mind was thinking. There are several reasons for this. There are different levels and types of thoughts happening all at once. There are thoughts you are aware of, such as what you are going to have for lunch, what the next task on your list is, or what you need to say to someone while listening to a conversation. Then there are thoughts under the surface that you don't pay attention to.

> *"A truly happy person is one who can enjoy the scenery while on a detour."*
>
> ~Author Unknown

When thinking about lunch, you may be thinking about your diet versus what you really are craving to eat. There are the tasks you need to accomplish, and subsequently challenges you face completing the tasks, or you may have fears/desires for the tasks to have a specific outcome. When talking with someone, you are listening and freely responding. However, in the background, you may be worried about what he/she will think of your answers, or maybe past experiences are coming to mind that are informing how you are responding.

Another issue that arises is we don't just think. We feel, we remember, we make connections, we develop opinions, and we pull from the past and project into the future. All of this is still in the area of *thoughts* our mind is generating. Your IGS is responding to all of this, and it may not be on the surface or easily accessible when, at first, you are unaware of how your mind works.

Additionally, we just are not conscious of our minds on a regular basis. Most of us just live and let our mind do what ever it wants. It is not like we were taught to pay attention to this powerful part of who we are. We did not know that we needed to, so we didn't in the past, thus setting up a pattern of disregarding paying attention to our mind and how it was operating, and now we don't have that ability in current time. This is why therapy is so powerful and important, since it gives us a chance to reflect on what we are thinking and question if it is actually how we would like to be thinking about things. As young children, most of us were not taught to listen to ourselves or to reflect on who we are inside.

When you begin to slow down, feel your body, and experience your IGS, a natural progression is to examine the opening and closing thoughts. It is a powerful path of self-discovery. The key is to not judge what you are thinking; do not worry about the content of closing thoughts. Just recognize that the guidance you are receiving is that the thought is not true and is not leading your toward great fulfillment and success. At this point choice begins to occur. When you find a closing thought, play with different perspectives and different ways of thinking about the situation, the person, or their motives. When one of these brings a sense of relief or opening, build upon that thought. Use the momentum of the opening to change how you are seeing things.

Please refer to the corresponding
exercise on the audio CD.

Emotions and Your IGS

Your emotions are not the same as your Internal Guidance System. Distinguishing between your emotions and your IGS is very important. In the beginning many people believe they are feeling an opening or a closing based on what they are feeling emotionally in a situation. This is not necessarily an inaccurate assumption in the beginning. Since most of us have linked the guidance provided by the IGS with emotions, you may find that in the beginning they often match. However, rather quickly in your journey you will find that they are not the same.

Your emotions are actually a biochemical reaction in the brain. Quite literally, you can think of them as if they were the

> *"Often people attempt to live their lives backwards; they try to have more things, or more money, in order to do more of what they want, so they will be happier. The way it actually works is the reverse. You must first be who you really are, then do what you need to do, in order to have what you want."*
>
> ~ Margaret Young

same as taking a drug, such as alcohol. If you think about times when you have been in the throws of an emotion, your ability to shift those emotions can be quite difficult. Even when the cause of the emotional experience is removed the residue of the energy is still present for quite some time. This is not the way your IGS behaves. Your IGS shifts and moves without any residue. Yes, for some it may seem like they are still feeling a closing after the cause is removed, but, if you really check in, the residue is from the leftover chemical that the brain has released in the form of the accompanied emotions.

At first what is most important is that you simply realize that when you are feeling emotional it will take time for the emotional chemistry that was released to dissolve. As you explore your IGS you will find that your emotions begin to be something that you are aware of, and that, quite simply, those emotions are just another piece of information for you to check with your IGS about. I have a perfect example of how this unfolded in my own life.

When I was a young woman I thought I was a jealous person. The response I had with my boyfriends sure seemed like jealousy. Well, I am not a person who sits by and lets some aspect of myself give others or me pain. I try to at least make peace with it. So off I went reading books, going to workshops, and trying on different aspects, perspectives, and practices to shift the jealousy I felt. Of course all of my boyfriends called my thoughts, feelings, and actions jealousy. I told them I was jealous. Why would they not believe me?

Then one day after years of failure around my issues of jealousy I was reading an article talking about insecurity. All of the symptoms I had attributed to jealousy were the same as insecurity. All of a sudden it hit me: I was insecure! What was most amazing about this realization is that when I had the thought that I was insecure my IGS rushed with energy, like it was a balloon with a hole in it. I got so excited that I immediately called my current boyfriend and excitedly told him how insecure I was. He promptly replied, "Uh, is this a trick question? Cause, well, didn't you know that?"

My point is that finding out I was not jealous, but instead that I was insecure, made all the difference. The way you deal with jealousy is very different from dealing with insecurity. Jealousy is about possessing or controlling someone, while insecurity is about self-worth. I had spent years trying to solve something that was not really my problem. Emotionally it seemed like the same thing. I realize that my IGS had been closed as I thought about being jealous. It never dawned on me that the thoughts about my being jealous were not true, nor that the horrible, anxiety-ridden feelings I was having about my being jealous were my IGS attempting to guide me. Needless to say, I embarked on a path to become more secure and to understand my self-worth, and I no longer endure the same emotional pain.

What is my point? In my path to solving my insecurity, there were many times when I felt the insecurity and I felt the opening as I thought to myself, "This is my insecurity, this is not something my boyfriend is doing to me or doing wrong." Even in the throws of my insecure inner tantrums, the openings led me to new thoughts, which healed that part of me.

As mentioned in a previous section: You can have pleasant and unpleasant emotions, yet your IGS is independent of the emotional chemicals that flood your body in response. As you learn to trust your IGS you can begin to ask yourself questions about the emotions you have. Start by figuring out what you are feeling, then, when you have named what you are feeling frustration, despair, abandonment, even hope, happiness, and peace, check in with your IGS to ensure that what you are experiencing is true and leading you toward fulfillment and success.

One last note on this. You may not understand how you could feel happiness and peace and yet not have an opening in your IGS. Have you ever really wanted to be in a relationship with someone and been really happy when he/she called or even when you were with him/her, yet had this tight uncomfortable feeling no matter how good things were going? Yep, that is what I am talking about. He/she just was not the one at the time, and your IGS was letting you know that your thoughts and feelings about him/her were not going to lead you toward fulfillment or success.

Please refer to the corresponding
exercise on the audio CD.

Using Your IGS for Time Management

You may wonder why I go from emotions to time management. I find time management to be one of the most emotional aspects of my life and in the lives of many others. Whether you are always on time or never on time, we all have stress and differing levels of anxiety. What I have found is that time management can be boiled down to all of the *should, have to, need to,* and *must* of our lives. Very rarely are any of us capable of shifting this to the *want to, love to,* and the ever-exciting *cannot wait to* be doing anything. Yes, of course we all go on vacations or have that rare afternoon where there is nothing else that is pressing, and we let ourselves indulge in the latter.

This is one of the best things you can use your IGS for, and it has changed my life and the lives of thousands of people! Your IGS, thank the heavens, is ever ready and present to help you enjoy and prioritize your to-do list into having a fulfilling and successful experience in life.

If your mind is anything like mine or my clients', then you know that on any given day it will give you a multitude of *should, have to, need to,* and *must.* You many have heard the phrase "stop should-ing on yourself." Well, this is where that phrase takes on new meaning. As you move through your day listening to the never-ending list of to-do items, your mind is running non-stop. As the thoughts race through your mind, notice your IGS and its guidance about what is a priority and what is not. You will find that many of the items on your running list are closing you. Now what exactly does that mean?

As I explained earlier in the chapter about where your IGS gets its guidance from, it sits outside of space and time. It is calculating what needs to happen and when it needs to happen. Think of it as your time-management traffic cop. It sends you signals regarding what is to happen next and then next and then next. It is so amazing that you will find that, when you let it do its magic, everything that needs to be done magically gets accomplished, and what does not need to be accomplished magically drops off your list.

This is how it works. As you go about your day and your mind begins running its list, you stop, feel your feet, breathe, and listen to the room around you. Then as you begin to run your list, again feel the guidance from your IGS. If you feel a closing about doing something, move to the next item until your IGS gives you an opening. This may sound tedious at first, but it soon becomes like second nature and you naturally will create your day this way.

You may be thinking, "Sure, I can do this in my personal life but in business, it is just not possible with all the demands I have on me, time lines, and accountabilities to others." Or you may be thinking, "Yeah, right. I am a parent. My time is not my own. I have practices, recitals, homework, cooking, cleaning, and making sure there is structure in my kid's life." No matter what the demands on your life are, I can tell you it works. I ran a multi-million-dollar business and got everything done. The only time there was pain was when I let my mind try to dictate my to-do list, rather than using my IGS.

When I was a consultant I had a project that had a tight time line. Every day I woke up and checked with my IGS about what to do that day, and I closed every time I thought about working on this project. This happened every day for ten days; the project had a fourteen-day time line. Needless to say I was starting to stress, which is the closing of my IGS. Each time my mind began running rampant about not getting the monumental amount of work accomplished, especially with the short time line, I realized I was closed. My thoughts were not true or leading me to success. This is very confusing if you attempt to use your logic.

I am a woman who walks her talk. Believe me, in the beginning it was challenging. On day ten, with still no opening to work on the project, I got a phone call. Let me tell you, I was not excited when I saw the company's number coming up on caller ID. The person on the phone asked me how much I had accomplished on the project. I honestly said, "I have not done anything. Every day I just felt like

I was not to be working on it yet." To my surprise there was relief in the person's voice. They said, "Thank God. We have just had a corporate meeting, our numbers are down, and we are going to scrap the entire project."

Much to my relief, my IGS stopped me from working on something that was not going to be fruitful. Yes, I would have been paid for my time, but what company wants to work with someone to whom they paid money for something they could not use? In the end they asked me to use the retainer to do another project, and everyone was happy. I woke up and had an opening to start working on the new project. That is the IGS at work.

> *"Map out your future, but do it in pencil."*
>
> ~ Jon Bon Jovi

I have story after story, just like this one, in my own life, and I have heard them from hundreds of others. It works. Using your IGS to help with your time management starts with you realizing that *any* time you are feeling stressed, rushed, or worried, you are *closed*. Yes, that is right: Your IGS is giving you closing sensations. *Stop* and look at what you are thinking about trying to cram in: picking up the dry cleaning, not having time to make dinner, being late for an appointment, cutting out time for yourself. It is endless, and we do this to ourselves every day.

When you feel the rushed sensation, realize that your IGS is asking you to take on a new perspective. For example, I am not supposed to do that now, or I will make it on time, or dinner will happen, or my part of the project will be ready just as it is needed. Feel if the new perspective creates an opening in your IGS; if it does, trust it! Move on to being present with your day, and allow the guidance you are receiving to support you in focusing on what counts. For more on this topic, download our free, 45-minute audio lesson.

You can find it at www.smartsoulacademy.com/timemanagement.

Urging from Your IGS

Not all of the sensations you receive from your IGS are in response to your thoughts. Independent of your thoughts, the IGS will give you what I like to call urgings. It is like when you feel an inner desire to take a new way home. Out of the blue you decide to go a different route, and you find that new amazing store, restaurant, or bookstore that you have been looking for. Another way that it informs you is when you get the feeling that you simply have to call a friend, and he/she was just thinking about you or needed you. You are about to leave the house and you feel the urge to grab a jacket, that item you need to return to the store, or your checkbook, and it turns out to be the exact thing you needed. Or you are leaving the house, get the urge, and ignore it, only to have to return later to retrieve the item you ignored the urge to grab. We all have these feelings but we don't necessarily give them much credit other than being coincidence.

I am here to let you know that these urgings are more than a coincidence, they are important, and they are to be listened to. This is not to say that we don't have urges that are addiction-related or are compulsions. The difference is whether your IGS is opened or closed, and whether those urges are combined with an unpleasant emotional sensation or are a habit. What I consider to be the urging of your IGS feels like an opening magnetic pull, which you may or may not agree with. The following example may help you to understand the difference.

> *"He who has faith has...an inward reservoir of courage, hope, confidence, calmness, and assuring trust that all will come out well—even though to the world it may appear to come out most badly."*
>
> ~ B.C. Forbes

I was preparing for a very, very long business trip. There was so much to do in a short afternoon. As I was going about accomplishing what needed to be completed, I kept getting the urging to go to my local coffee shop, Peet's. Peet's has long been a cosmic place for me, with meeting friends and amazing experiences happening when I am there. On that particular afternoon I had no time for it. At first I discounted the opening urging as simply my desire to not be packing and getting the house battened down for my long departure.

> *"Faith is a passionate intuition."*
>
> ~ William Wordsworth

Quickly I began to realize that my IGS was giving me stronger and more insistent messages to go to Peet's to get coffee. The funny thing is that I started getting frustrated with my IGS. You too will experience this—almost like arguing with a child. I did not even want a coffee! Fine, I decided. I would get it out of the way. Off I went to get coffee. I got my coffee, and, as I was leaving the shop, I started to close. When I checked my thoughts, I realized that I was thinking of heading home to the checklist still needing to be completed to go on my trip. When I thought about staying, sitting, and drinking my coffee, I opened. I was really annoyed, but I have learned that, if I don't listen to my IGS, the outcome will not be positive. So I went over to the bar stools facing the window and sat down, pretty much in a huff even though I am opening. The woman next to me started chatting about what I do and I thought, "Oh, cosmic Peet's, maybe this is why I am here," but the thought closed me.

We chatted for a few minutes, and I saw a friend of mine who lives at least 20 miles away walking across the street. She got her coffee, and I turned around to surprise her and say hello. The woman I had just been talking to turned back to the window and her newspaper. I asked my girlfriend why she was in the area, and she unleashed a rush of excitement. She told me that she just graduated from school and was applying for a job as a counselor for this abused children's center (she gave me the name), and that this was a very important interview. She was so inspired by the work this children's center was doing that she went to school specifically because she wanted to work with this particular center. It was a dream of hers.

The woman that I had been talking with turned around with a shocked look on her face and stated, "I am the one who is going to be interviewing you." You cannot imagine the look on both of their faces. My friend got a chance with absolute authenticity to gush about her passion and excitement. The two of them began talking, and I suddenly had an urging to return home to finish my packing. I got everything done, made my plane on time, and got to be a part of some Divine plan to bring these two together in a very different way than they intended. She attained the position.

The urgings given to you by your IGS will not always make sense, and you will not always see the immediate results, like I mention above. Sometimes you will get an urge to take a nap, spend more time with your cat, or simply drive a different way home. Over the years I have found that the miracles both great and small have come from following these precious internal openings.

> *"You must train your intuition—you must trust the small voice inside you which tells you exactly what to say, what to decide."*
>
> ~ Ingrid Bergman

Please refer to the corresponding
exercise on the audio CD.

Asking Direct Questions

As a rule I don't recommend you sit and just ask questions of your IGS. Working with hundreds of clients, I have found that they get stuck asking about everything in their lives instead of living. Your IGS is a guidance system that works best when you are living your life. Just like a GPS in a car: You can sit there parked in the car just punching in destinations, yet never moving. Sure, you will get a response that it knows the way, but until you start actually driving, most of the features of the GPS are not functioning. As you go about your day, checking in and feeling your IGS as you are planning, organizing, and dealing with your life, works the very best.

> *"The self is not something ready-made, but something in continuous formation through choice of action."*
>
> ~ John Dewey

The mind will often start a zealous quest to "know" everything—asking, "Should I do this or should I do that? Is this the right person for me? Is it in my highest purpose to leave my job? Would this area be best for me to live in?" Most often your IGS gives you what you need to know, as you need to know it. It knows what is just the right amount of guidance and what is too much so that you will zoom ahead and get yourself off track. Sometimes there is not enough information available or all the puzzle pieces have not fallen into place yet for your IGS to give you guidance. If you can *visualize* moving down a specific path, picturing or feeling it, and wondering about it, you will have better openings and closings than asking single or specific questions.

Questions vs. Statements

If you are going to ask for specific information from time to time, then you need to find out how to ask for information. For some reason, some people are question people and some are statement people—and some are both. I recommend testing yourself to discover which gives you a better opening response. It is quite simple: Just ask as you did in the sample exercise at the beginning of the book to feel your IGS section. Quiet your mind by feeling you feet, breathe, and listen to the area around you, then slowly ask, "Am I a question person?" Wait for a response. "Am I a statement person?" Wait for a response. "Am I both?" Which did you get the biggest response to? You will get a more consistent opening and closing if you understand what your IGS responds to most effectively.

The first step in asking questions of the IGS is always quieting your mind using your feet, breathing, and listening. Then develop the ability to focus on one thought at a time. If this seems "easy," take a moment to identify a question you *need* an answer to (for instance, it may be a question regarding your career, relationship, or financial situation), and then watch the background noise rush at you. Each of these areas above has so much associated with them, including beliefs, memories, future projections, and/or fear. When you ask the question, your mind will present all the existing pro and con arguments.

That is what the mind is supposed to do, right? Since your IGS is attempting to guide you on your thoughts, when you have multiple thoughts racing around, you are getting guidance on the bulk of them, and things can become confusing and unclear.

Using Imagination to Receive Guidance from the IGS

Visualizing or thinking of a scenario playing out is a more effective way to receive guidance from your IGS. A great way to do this is to run a scenario of what you are planning to do through your mind and see if you open or close. Try not to get too descriptive; keep it simple. For example, you might picture yourself going to an event, calling upon a client, working on a project, or reading at home alone.

If your scenarios become too complex—if, for example, rather than picturing an event, you picture yourself, the event, all the people, what you planned to wear, the food you anticipate eating at the event, and the people you expect to see, this would be too much information. Keep it simple and isolate your thoughts. If you are not strong in visualizing and, like me, are a feeling or sensation person (who would have guessed?), then another approach you could take is to imagine what the situation would feel like and see if your IGS opens or closes.

Please refer to the corresponding
exercise on the audio CD.

Four Powerful Questions

Four powerful questions, listed below, will save you a great deal of time and energy in working with your IGS, and will keep you from letting emotional or unpleasant situations take over your life. I recommend approaching any situation of even mild importance with these questions as a way to weed through what truly needs your attention and what does not.

You can reduce a lot of stress and the occurrence of closing thoughts by using these four questions:

1. Is this any of my business?
2. Is the thought I am having truthful?
3. Is there anything I need to do about this situation right now?
4. Do I have all the information I need to act right now?

If you receive opening sensations to each of these questions, you can trust that it is right to take action. The experience of navigating the situation with the guidance of your IGS will most likely be rewarding and fulfilling for you and those around you. If you get a closing to any of these questions, then you do not need to be concerned. You can trust that you will know when to do something, or it will just not be an issue that is yours to deal with.

"We are wiser than we know."

~ Ralph Waldo Emerson

Is This Any of My Business?

This question is my favorite. I love when I ask this question and I get a closing. It means that I can go about my own business and that the situation does not need me. *Always* ask this question about *everything.* You will be absolutely shocked at how little you receive an opening sensation that it is your business. Even things about ourselves, our family, work, and very seemingly personal things will receive a closing. Why, you might ask? Our time is so limited, our focus so precious, and our energy limited, so it is important to put our time, focus, and energy where they matter. Each and every day there are situations trying to take up these three valuable commodities. To have such a simple question will allow us to release what is not ours to do and allow us to keep moving forward with what is important to us. This becomes a most wonderful gift.

Is the Thought I Am Having Truthful?

Have you ever questioned your thoughts? Questioned how accurate they are? In an instant, our mind makes conclusions about a multitude of thoughts. When that happens, off we go with that instantaneous assumption. If something is my business (I am usually disappointed to find out it is), I then go to this question next. Why? It is crucial to make sure what you are thinking and how you are thinking about something is accurate. Here is a little story that will give you an example of what I mean.

I was at a friend's home for a party. The living room was fairly large, and from where I was sitting I could see the front door and who was arriving. A good friend of mine arrived, and, when she looked at me, she glared at me for a few seconds, did not smile, and then turned to enter the kitchen. Having experienced the horrors of being excluded in elementary school, you can guess where my mind instantly went: What did I do wrong? Why is she angry with me? For the next two hours, I talked with other people. My mind, however, was reeling, going over the last time this woman and I spoke, what I said, and if there was anything I could have done differently. I came up with a multitude of things that might have triggered this good friend not talking to me. Finally, after being completely tortured by this process and feeling horrible inside, I went to find out what her problem was.

She was still in the kitchen. In fact, she had not moved since she got there. I walked up to her and as I got closer she gave me a bright smile, which totally confused me. She grabbed my arm and pulled me next to her to whisper in my ear, "Who is the person in the blue shirt standing over in the dining room?" I looked through the doorway in to the dimmer room and told her it was a mutual friend, to which she replied that it was who she thought it was. I looked at her like she was crazy. She confided in me that she did not have her contacts in, and that she had left her glasses in her other purse. She was in such a rush when her ride came that she completely forgot to take them. She could not see clearly more than a few feet and was memorizing the colors people were wearing so she could identify them.

She was not glaring at me; she was blind! How silly I felt wasting so much time fretting. The most interesting part is I was *closed* the entire time, but my mind was so convinced that the glaring look meant she was angry with me. I never even questioned that very first assumption: Was it true she was angry with me? Since then I have learned to check my very, very first assumption. You can prevent so much drama if you ask this question and trust the answer.

Is There Anything I Need to Do About This Situation Right Now?

Once you know something is your business *and* that what you are thinking about the situation is accurate, you can move on to this next question. Additionally, at this point you have received an opening to the previous questions. If you have not, don't go on to this question; it is not necessary. However, now you need to know about timing. Is the timing right for you do anything? If you get an opening, then you can move on to the last question. If you close, that simply means to relax and wait, because the timing is not right regarding what needs to happen next, and when it is the solution will naturally occur.

If you doubt this, simply visualize (preferably) your knowing exactly what to do and when. You don't have to picture the exact solutions, just the feeling of the issue being pleasantly resolved. If you open, you can be certain that all is moving along just fine. If you cannot visualize, then you can ask. Feel your feet, breathe, listen to the area around you, and, when your mind is focused on these things, hold the thought "I will know what to do when the time comes." I have always gotten an opening if I hold the thought singularly and in a focused way. It is an effective way to help your mind relax.

A note on the steps to quieting your mind: The process, with practice, is instantaneous. As you get comfortable with it, it literally takes one to three seconds. It essentially begins to happen all at once and becomes a set point for communicating with your IGS.

Do I Have All the Information I Need to Act Right Now?

The last question in the series is needed only if you know that it is your business, that what you are thinking is true, and that the time to do something in the situation is now. You want to be sure you have all the information you need to find, provide, or facilitate a solution. If you ask this question and you close, slow down. The reason is that you don't have all the information you need to act. (How you will know this is that you opened to the last question, so the solution is not clear.) Enter the situation in a humble state. If there is something that is expected for you to do, then let others know that you don't have the answers but are there to help to figure things out. What this means is that things will unfold. Usually the solution is a collaborative effort, with various people contributing their part.

> *"The art of knowing is knowing what to ignore."*
>
> ~ Rumi

With these four questions you gain insight that will support you in being wise and effective. Your IGS will guide you the rest of the way, and most of the problems that create drama in our lives can been avoided.

Troubleshooting

Section Three

Asking Too Many Questions

As mentioned in the previous section, I don't recommend people ask questions of their IGS directly. Your IGS has so much more knowledge about you, your life, and what direction will make you the happiest. You may not have clarity about the best direction to select due to your thoughts being creatively limited. What do I mean by that? Let's say that you are opening around the idea that it is time to move to another location, but you are not sure where. As you research the area neighborhoods, nothing elicits anything but a neutral sensation. When you start asking your IGS additional questions regarding possible areas to move to, you get closings and neutrals but no openings. Often at that point you start getting confused and begin to second-guess the opening you have around moving at all.

Most likely, the issue is not your opening being false, but your questioning moving is in the wrong direction. What if your greatest fulfillment and success is to move 500 miles away—but if things are not lined up yet for that move, and there is an offer coming soon but you don't know it, then you will not get the response you're expecting to receive. This type of thing has happened to many people using their IGS. This situation happened to me.

I knew I had to move—it was time to leave my apartment—and I still had no idea where I was moving. At the last moment an opportunity became available. I moved to a place that I would have never even thought of, and it was there where I met my new husband. Had I not followed my opening to move, I have no idea how my IGS would have gotten us together. Your IGS cannot give you an opening unless you are having the thoughts.

So expand your imagination, dream bigger, look at what you would love to have happen most, and be available for the unexpected. When holding these thoughts, not questions, notice if you are opened or closed. Dreaming and visualizing are the best ways to get the most accurate answers from your IGS, not by direct questions.

The Frozen Mind: Changing the Channel

Often beginning students report finding themselves locked in a thought pattern where their mind will not let it go. This usually happens with big emotional situations in life. It could be a fight with a friend or relative, cutbacks at your job, a breakup or divorce, custody battles, or health issues—traumatic issues, depending on the possible outcome you might face. Your mind goes into protective overdrive attempting to solve this issue, or it has a compulsion to keep working on the problem, looking for a solution. Very often when this happens the IGS gives full-throttle closing sensations. It can feel very uncomfortable while it guides you to not thinking about the problem in the way that you are. When you change your thinking, you change the outcome.

Once you know what a closing sensation means, this creates even more discomfort. The important thing to remember is that the thoughts you are having are closing and are not true. First remember to hold that thought over and over. If your mind will still not break free from the habitual thoughts, then you must learn to *change the channel*. The mind has a challenging time focusing on more than a few things at a time. This is why focusing on your feet, breathing, and listening help to calm your mind. This is the same tactic to use with your frozen mind.

It is important that you do something you enjoy that will take your mind off of the issue. Call a friend, reach out to help someone else, go to a movie, read a book, go exercise, or throw yourself into a creative activity that you love.

What seems to work most is to do something that opens up your physical and creative energy. For me, what works is listening to high-energy music, going jogging, or calling friends whom I have been unable to catch up with. This gives my mind so much more to think about than the problems it is focused upon.

When you are facing this situation, it can be very helpful to have two lists to refer to: a list of activities that engage you, and a list of friends to call. Your mind may not be very creative or helpful in changing the channel, so a list can help clarify powerful actions to take. Make sure the list is filled with ideas that are physically or emotionally stimulating. Possibilities like knitting, meditation, or watching TV may not be enough to have your mind shift gears.

Pushing to Change the Response from Your IGS

Along the same theme as the frozen mind is when your mind begins to feel that it has to find an answer to some question or situation. It will begin to ask the same question over and over and over, getting a neutral or a closing, yet not wanting those to be the answers. It is funny how your mind can actually argue against you, not believe the guidance you are receiving, or have the guidance given by the IGS be rejected. What can happen is that you will come back and think about the situation again. Very often this can happen when you really want something and your IGS is giving you guidance that is closed about it.

For example, let's say you are dating someone, and you are being guided that the relationship is over. It opens you when you think about being complete with this person, and each time you go to call him/her, see him/her, or think about staying together, there is a closing sensation. Just because your IGS is guiding you to end the romantic relationship does not mean emotionally you want that to occur. What can happen is your mind and IGS start negotiating with each other: Well, what if we just sleep together, or we can still be friends, it's just dinner, or maybe I can still talk to them. The good thing about your IGS is that it is consistent. You may feel like calling the person, and as you go to dial you feel the closing. You phone him/her anyway and he/she answers. It seems that the conversation goes well for a few minutes, and then something happens. One of you says something that triggers the other, and strong words and fighting begin. Finally you end the conversation and hang up thinking, "Why did I not listen to my IGS."

It won't be the last time you don't listen to your IGS, but each time you learn to trust the closing, you will have confidence in it more and more. Eventually you will trust it enough that you will not even pick up the phone, and you will let go of things more quickly, knowing your IGS is truly moving you toward greater fulfillment and success. This is just a process that everyone goes through, so just go through it. Trust the process. The faster you realize the guidance works, the faster you will not get caught in this loop.

Not Trusting the Neutral

Neutral is very frustrating when you first begin working with your IGS. Neutral does not feel like anything, and there is an expectation that something will be felt. Remember: Your IGS is not a yes/no system but more like a compass. Neutral is part of the guidance that your IGS gives.

Many people believe their IGS is not working or that something is wrong. This is not the case at all. When you get a neutral it only means that you have not hit upon the thought that is moving you in any particular direction, that there is no guidance on the thoughts that you are having, or that you are thinking too many thoughts at once for your IGS to isolate any particular one to give you guidance. The first two reasons given above are easy to understand. The third one can be a bit elusive, so I will explain that one in more detail.

> *"It is the heart always that sees, before the head can see."*
>
> ~Thomas Carlyle

If you are thinking many contradictory things at once then your IGS will often just go to neutral, while your mind calms. If you have too many choices going in too many differing directions and none of them are really a fit for what will bring you the highest degree of fulfillment or success, you will get the neutral guidance.

A perfect example of this is a college student attempting to pick a major. Looking at the course catalog, he/she goes through each item, and nothing seems to bring an opening or closing as guidance. The best course of action could be just a general course of study for a period of time as the student explores various topics. The neutral is because there is not guidance to pick a major. If the student were to hold the thought that it is not time to pick a major, he/she very likely would get an opening. You will be surprised at how often there is nothing to be done in the moment.

Compulsively Reversing Questions When in Doubt

I must admit that this trouble spot comes from the very first exercise I give people to experience their IGS. Remember making the statements "I do not have an Internal Guidance System" and "I do have an Internal Guidance System"? What occurs is people begin asking questions both ways, "Am I to go to this event tonight? Am I not to go to this event tonight?" This can work fine if you do this once. However, students get into the habit of doing this with everything, thus becoming a habit for the mind to do on its own. Going back and forth, and back and forth, does not work and will drive you crazy. The IGS actually shuts down—literally goes into a lockdown. I cannot emphasize enough how constant back-and-forth questions are problematic when using your IGS. The issue is not your IGS but your mind. When you really doubt yourself or the answers your IGS is giving you, that doubt becomes the reason for asking questions both ways.

So think about it. What are the underlying thoughts that are actually being produced by your mind? *Doubt.* Since you have felt and experienced that the IGS is real, what will you get from your IGS when in doubt? A closing or a neutral. The closing will be due to the thoughts of doubt; the neutral will be because there are too many conflicting thoughts running around in your mind. If you want to "tune up" your IGS return to the original statements: "I do not have an IGS. I do have an IGS." However, it is best not to do that in an attempt to prove what guidance you are given.

I have recommended to students to visualize one situation and then to visualize it going the opposite way. This can support your confidence in moving forward. It can be helpful to reverse the question once and see if you receive an opposite response. Over time I recommend not doing this. As your trust in your IGS builds and you get used

Troubleshooting

to its guidance being accurate, drop this approach. What works much better is when you receive guidance on a thought or visualization and then ask if you just had an opening or a closing. Stating "I just received an opening" will produce a continuation of the opening.

Most importantly if you find yourself doing this—sometimes our mind just does it whether we like it or not—then attempt to use the change the channel method. Take control of your thoughts as best you can, or you may find yourself very confused and damaging the trust you have created thus far. As you move forward with guidance from your IGS, this will eventually stop. You will have so many instances when your IGS was right that you will just relax more and more.

81

Closing Is Just Closing

Once people understand what the closing sensation means, they often start judging themselves for being closed. Being closed is not something to be concerned with. It is just closing—a form of guidance that provides you with choice. That is all! It does not mean that you are bad, wrong, or in trouble. In some cases, some of us were raised that, if we are wrong or make a mistake, we are *bad*. If you use your sense of reason, you have figured out that it is through trial and error that we learn. *Error* is not a bad word; it is just part of our learning process.

Your IGS is providing you with feedback about whether your thoughts are going to end up being the most powerful ones that will get you to where you most desire to be. If you find that you are feeling shame or embarrassment, or feel like hiding or lying about when you are closed, you are not alone. Most of us who are exploring this new, powerful part of ourselves feel that way, especially if there is emotion or ego attached. Just remind yourself that closing is part of the experience—that it is actually a gift and is a very important part of your gathering information that will help you succeed. Admit as often as possible that you are closed. Start with little things and gradually let yourself openly admit it to your friends, loved ones, and professional associates. Amazingly, the honesty generates trust, respect, and admiration.

It can look something like this. "I have been arguing that we are pricing our services too high, yet I now am closed (or actually feel like I am not correct) when I think of it that way. There is part of me that thinks people will not hire us because our work is too costly. Can we discuss this again?" You would be so surprised how many times I have argued for something adamantly and then suddenly had to change course when I realized I was totally receiving a closing. Then I felt embarrassed and had to force myself to change directions. The most amazing thing is that, when I actually admit that is what is happening for me, the people around me are amazed at my ability to communicate that, and greater trust is created. Closing is just closing; it is what you do with the closing once you recognize it that counts.

Don't Panic if You Followed the Closing

The closing sensation does not mean that you are going to be unfulfilled and unsuccessful. This is a common rationalization that comes to mind when you realize suddenly you are following your closing. Let's say you are in an argument with your partner. He/she did something that set your mind off in a closing direction. This happens very often when you are learning to access your IGS. The old patterns in your relationship still arise until you have a chance to realize that they close you.

Here's a situation: Your partner comes home late from work and the two of you have somewhere you need to be. Your mind jumps to how many problems his/her being late is going to cause. Your mind may sound something like this: "Great. Now we are going to hit traffic, and we are going to miss the beginning of the event. Everyone is going to notice when we walk in the door late. We are going to be seen as flaky. He/she doesn't even have time to really dress properly for the event. I hate it when this happens!" Soon after a fight with your partner ensues.

The interesting thing about this is, if all of this were true, you would be open. What naturally happens when you open is that you feel calm and relaxed so you are able to handle the situation; you are focused and easy-going. The issue does not cause a fight or tension. The tension arises when you are closed. After the fight you realize that you are closed, meaning that your thoughts about what is going to happen are not true.

Don't panic because you let your closing get out of control. Go back and think of the situation from the perspective of not being late or that your being late will actually end up being on time. (Numerous times I've shown up just when people are ready for

Troubleshooting

me.) Play with the thoughts and find the opening. You may need to apologize to your partner and tell them you will try to check with your IGS sooner next time.

Believe me, I still have trouble with this type of thing. My mind is so great at generating the worst-case scenario, and it is so real, that I forget to notice whether I am closed or open. Don't be concerned or panicked if you have followed the closing. In every moment your IGS is right there, ready to bring you back to the thoughts and path that will lead toward fulfillment and success. You are always only a few opening thoughts away from being on track. It is simply a matter of looking for what opens you.

Keep in Motion

Your IGS is an action-loving system—not that it will not guide you toward relaxing when you need to, but it works most effectively when you are going about your life. There are times when someone will contact me because of indecision regarding what to do when he/she is stuck. What I tell the person is to get moving, in any direction. Your IGS is always sending you guidance. Once you start in a direction, you will begin to feel your IGS giving you sensations as guidance.

> *"In the midst of movement and chaos, keep stillness inside of you."*
>
> ~ Deepak Chopra

There may be a decision that you are unsure of. You will know right away as you move forward because your IGS does not give you guidance to move in any direction. Your IGS will be there all along the way, guiding you on all the little details, decisions and ideas you have about how to accomplish what you have opened to. Or it will give you a closed signal until you listen.

By keeping in motion, you are generating thoughts in the form of choices, planning, ideas, and connections to be made. Imagine your IGS paying attention to the situation so it can support you in making the most powerful decisions. If you cannot decide what to do, then get into motion on something! If you are thinking you need to switch careers, start getting your resume together and look at what other things you might like to do. You will find that you open at writing your resume, or you are closed. As you sit down to write it will feel like a struggle, or you will be happily humming along enjoying the experience. It really is just that easy.

The IGS Rarely Leads You Directly from Point A to Point B

An opening or a closing does not mean that that is what is going to happen in your life. If you open to moving, you may not actually move in the end. This may sound confusing unless you understand that your IGS is doing its best to move you toward greater fulfillment and success. *You* are sometimes what is in the way of that happening. Its job is not to provide you with stability, but instead to bring you toward happiness. Often the way your IGS exhibits its response is by taking you in one direction so you can accomplish what you will need to accomplish, and then it may need to take you in a completely new direction.

One of my coaching clients had a rather dramatic experience with this. She was living on the East Coast, and her family lived on the West Coast. As we were looking for her next steps in life she opened at moving to be near her family. At the time she was a business owner, was of retirement age, and had a boyfriend and a home that she owned. She was tired of working so hard and caring for all the things in her life. She set about taking care of all the things that needed to happen so that she could move, using her IGS all along the way.

She sold all of her inventory and did not renew the lease on her business location. Her business transformed into consulting work that thrilled her and was work that could be done anywhere she lived. She broke up with her longtime boyfriend, not wanting to have a long-distance relationship. Her home sold so quickly that she had to rent a cute little apartment while she finished getting everything organized for her big move. The apartment would not hold all of her belongings, and, since she was moving, she decided to simplify by selling items she no longer wanted.

At that point it was summer and she began calling all of her old friends to spend time with them before she left. Suddenly, out of the blue she realized what opened her was to stay living where she was. When she thought of moving, it closed her. When we spoke about it in the next coaching session, she had a new clarity and joy in her voice. The move to the West Coast was just a carrot at the end of a stick. If her IGS had given her a list of things she would need to do to be truly fulfilled in her life, it would have been overwhelming. However, one carrot accomplished everything. She still lives very happily and simply on the East Coast today.

You may start a course of study, get halfway through it, and get an opening sensation to stop the course. Another way to look at it is that you gained what you needed to learn. There are so many paths to get to where you are going. Your IGS is going to get you there as simply and painlessly as it can. As you stay with the guidance this will get more and more comfortable for you. Remember: If you are asked to stop something or go in a different direction than what you opened to in the beginning, your IGS will be there sending you openings and closings all along the way.

You Cannot Trick Your IGS

A common question I get is: "Can you trick your IGS?" The answer is no. Yes, you can play with your thoughts to get an opening or a closing. However, as I mentioned earlier, as you proceed down a path, your IGS will let you know if you are on course or not. One example of this is a woman who really wanted to be with the man who had broken up with her. When she sat and imagined being back with him, she would close. So she began to imagine being in love, traveling the world in love, and moving into an amazing apartment with her love. All of this opened her, but the thought of him closed her. She told me about how she felt she could trick her IGS into opening.

What was really happening is that she was imagining him out of all the pictures, and she opened. Her mind then let itself believe it was about him. Within a year she was in love with a different man, was traveling to various foreign locations, and they had moved in together. Everything she imagined that opened her showed up in her life—with the right person for her.

> *"Only do what your heart tells you."*
> ~ Princess Diana

Your mind is a powerful tool, as is your IGS. Your deepest desires will almost always open you if they are really your authentic desires. Those are the dreams that your IGS is already hard at work leading you toward. If there is a dream that is not truly what you desire, you will close to it no matter how hard you try. There are people who study their IGS and believe their dream is a high-paying career, an expensive car, and a multi-million-dollar home. As they begin to build a relationship with their IGS, they often find that these things may not open them. What they want are freedom, travel, and to pursue a passion. The aforementioned things are what they believe they need to have before they can do what they are really dreaming of. This is a common mistake. Your IGS is leading directly in the most efficient way to your greatest fulfillment and success.

Conclusion

Section Four

Conclusion

> "There is a vitality, a life force, a quickening that is translated through you into action and because there is only one of you in all time, this expression is unique.
>
> And if you block it, it will never exist through any other medium and will be lost. The world will not have it. It is not your business to determine how good it is nor how valuable it is nor how it compares with other expressions. It is your business to keep it yours clearly and directly, to keep the channel open.
>
> You do not even have to believe in yourself or your work. You have to keep open and aware directly to the urges that motivate you.
>
> Keep the channel open."
>
> ~ Martha Graham

"Be the Change You Wish to See in the World"

Mahatma Gandhi once instructed his devotees to "be the change you wish to see in the world." His point was not to identify the problems of the world and kvetch over the shortcomings of humanity. Rather, he advocated an active practice of embodying the higher qualities of being each of us desires to see in the people around us.

With a cultivation of your IGS, you have a tool to help you to "be the change you wish to see." The IGS will help you to true yourself up to a perspective that is different but more rewarding than the habitual, reactionary one that most of us perpetuate. By focusing on and following opening sensations, you align yourself with a perspective that is conscious and creative, and is a source of new solutions from a deeper form of intelligence. As you will find, many miracles will then occur.

Every Day Sacred

The practice of using your IGS is about making every day sacred and supporting yourself to move from fear, worry, anxiety, stress, and reaction to a state of clarity, peace, and empowerment regardless of what is happening in your particular situation.

Your lifetime holds many different levels of purpose and destiny. One of the highest levels, I believe, is in living within a mindset that every day is sacred. For me, "every day sacred" means expanding and moving into opening sensations as a means of service to something higher than myself. It means moving out of the fear, worry, anxiety, stress, reactivity, power plays, and problems, and into accessing the eternal sacredness in every moment.

> *"We cannot live for ourselves alone. Our lives are connected by a thousand invisible threads, and along these sympathetic fibers, our actions run as causes and return to us as results."*
>
> ~ Herman Melville

As you practice this, at some point you will find yourself moving from stage one to stage two of using the IGS. In this book, I have introduced you to the first stage, in which you notice and feel the sensations of the IGS. At some point, you will naturally move to stage two, in which you live in the flow of opening sensations from moment to moment. When you're moving from stage one to stage two, you move from "Oh! I'm feeling and noticing something" to "There's something else going on here; on a moment-to-moment basis, I am feeling flowing energy coming and going through me into the world, and it is creating peace, goodness, and balance." That flow will lead you toward becoming a symbiotic part of the world around you.

Conclusion

Every day you will notice a growing sense of confidence that you are a part of the whole and that you cherish your part without feeling the need to overemphasize it or deflate it. You will have become a living example of grace and compassion.

I can't tell you how many times I have picked up the phone to talk to my business partner and realize she is already on the phone before I could even dial, because she has just called me. Or I call her about a specific document, and she was holding it in her hand as she went to pick up the phone. You may have noticed these types of instances in your life, and, as you move more deeply into stage two of your IGS, you will notice these instances happening more frequently to a point in which you are in a flow with others and life itself. What is exciting is that this way of being is available to *everyone*; it simply takes the practice of cultivating the IGS to make being in the flow as natural as breathing.

> *"Some luck lies in not getting what you thought you wanted, but getting what you have, which once you have got it, you may be smart enough to see is what you would have wanted had you known."*
>
> ~ Garrison Keillor

The alternative is to stay disconnected from ourselves, focused on our imperfections and those of others. I like to think of our closings as unpleasant triggers that are being set off so we are reminded that we have a choice regarding where we focus our energy and attention.

My trigger causes your trigger, which causes a whole new level of communication that would never have occurred if we were just running around in paradise, having fun together. That trigger is exactly what we need to grow and evolve—to become richer, deeper, and more aligned with our highest self, our highest truth, and our deepest joy.

"Every Day Sacred" Does Not Equal "Every Day Perfect"

The expression of making every day sacred is adopting a point of view, a perspective, and a way of being that allows your IGS to show you the jagged edges that need to be polished so that your gleaming diamond of Self can emerge.

This practice is about bringing sacred awareness into your everyday life. It is *not* about being perfect, according to your ego. It happens when you're messy and when you don't do it well. In addition, it's not about being perfect and conscious all the time; it is about being conscious when you're not perfect, and being conscious and present enough to find your opening thoughts. Over time you will increase your level of consciousness and capacity to remain present and, as you do, you will be able to focus on the opening and move toward divine collaboration with others—collaboration that leads to the furthering of love, joy, compassion, and forgiveness on the planet. Following your opening thoughts naturally supports you in being a part of this collaboration.

I believe we came out of paradise so that we can re-choose it with a greater level of appreciation and depth. Part of what we're experiencing is learning to understand what we don't want, so that we can have the integrity and perseverance to move away from pain and fear, and toward the creation of a new form a paradise, one in which we are all conscious contributors. I believe this is the point of evolution where we are now.

Conclusion

Enjoying the Process

I recommend we all remember to enjoy the process, because turning the earth back into paradise is a part of everyone's purpose, and it is a beautiful point in the evolution of humanity that is only available to those who are living *now*. We are at a point in which we can experience a deeper richness in being, a point at which we can develop healthier and more empowering relationships, a point at which human beings can allow a deeper level of intimacy, and a point at which we can practice "every day sacred."

> *"When the Japanese mend broken objects, they aggrandize the damage by filling the cracks with gold. They believe that when something's suffered damage and has a history it becomes more beautiful."*
>
> ~ Barbara Bloom

The Internal Guidance System is playing a large role in all of this, as it instructs each of us—among millions and millions of human beings—toward our highest good and the fulfillment of our highest potential. It is giving each of us access to a new source of wisdom and intelligence.

Through this new point of view, we also have access to a greater level of compassion—compassion for everyone in the world, including ourselves. As we work with the IGS, we learn to stop self-critical thoughts or those that are condemning of others and ourselves. We begin to see that these thoughts create unnecessary pain and so, as we interrupt them more quickly and frequently, their hold on us starts to expire. We begin to notice that we are opened by expressions of compassion and acceptance of our human form, as well as appreciation of our willingness to contribute our energy into the opening regardless of the fears of our mind/ego.

If you can remember nothing else, remember to have compassion for yourself as you move through the process, and remember that thinking thoughts that close you is the gateway to new growth and expansion of being.

> *"A human being is part of a whole, called by us the Universe, a part limited in time and space. He experiences himself, his thoughts and feelings, as something separated from the rest a kind of optical delusion of his consciousness. This delusion is a kind of prison for us, restricting us to our personal desires and to affection for a few persons nearest us. Our task must be to free ourselves from this prison by widening our circles of compassion to embrace all living creatures and the whole of nature in its beauty."*
>
> ~Albert Einstein

You have heard many teachers tell you that the answer to your woes is self-mastery, being present, or following your inner Truth. Absolutely do this! Except this time, do so with the confidence that you have a tool—a built-in sense—that can guide you firmly and lovingly into the direction of your spiritual evolution and highest good.

Thank you, thank you, thank you for learning about your IGS so you can create from your openings a fulfilled and successful life.

Are you ready to master your IGS?

Smart Soul Academy is the fastest way to build a successful understanding and relationship with your IGS®.

This is a powerful virtual online academy that allows you to attend lectures, be in a intimate learning team, participate in live coaching with Zen DeBrücke and discover simple practices that are guaranteed to build your ability to use your IGS® in every situation in your life.

Some of the benefits of being in the Academy:

- Recognize what is Authentic for you in ALL situations
- Release stress, ease, anxiety and fear; each used as a resource for guidance
- Stabilize your emotions and feelings
- Rid yourself of behavioral triggers that lead to blow ups and break downs
- Replace fear and worry with confident knowing, dissolve doubt
- Experience Sadness, frustration and discouragement as opportunities

You can actually embody as a natural response in your every day life the following benefits:

- Being present

- Happy
- Calm under pressure
- Having a sense of humor when things are tough
- A flow, ease and synchronicity that most people call miracles

Get a discount off of your enrollment in Smart Soul Academy when you use this code upon sign up: book2010gift

About the Author

Zen DeBrücke is an inspirational teacher and speaker and the creator of Smart Soul Academy. Smart Soul Academy is a unique combination of an online training system with offline support. It is made up of individuals with the ability to be present to the continuous guidance that is being provided by their Internal Guidance System (IGS). This unique, factory-installed system creates one's ability to receive consistent, successful results in life. The Academy and Zen's upcoming book, "Get Out of the Way Your Life is Coming at You: a Soul's Guide to Traversing Interesting Times" provide the practices and inspiration to live authentically as joy and truth.

A successful entrepreneur and business executive, Zen has coached hundreds of business leaders to use their IGS for success in every area of their lives. Zen recently joined the Transformational Leadership Council, which includes luminaries such as Jack Canfield, Marianne Williamson, John Gray and Michael Beckwith. Zen resides in Boulder Colorado and is a part of the Social Venture Network. Zen is known for her earlier work as the CEO of The Netkitchen, an Internet strategy-consulting firm, where she spent four years creating innovative internet campaigns and properties for Fortune 500 companies, including Applied Materials, IBM, Electronic Arts and VISA. She has also contributed to Delta Airlines as the media expert for their in-flight radio program and was a contributing editor to In-Radio Magazine.